Prayer journal

DATE _____

TODAY'S PASSAGE   PRE,

NOTES _____

KEY VERSES

PRAYER _____

KEY POINTS

APPLICATION

Prayer journal

DATE _____

TODAY'S PASSAGE _____   PREACHER _____   SERMON TOPIC _____

NOTES
_____
_____
_____
_____
_____
_____
_____
_____
_____
_____
_____
_____
_____

KEY VERSES

PRAYER
_____
_____
_____
_____
_____
_____

KEY POINTS

_____
_____
_____
_____
_____
_____
_____
_____
_____
_____

APPLICATION

Prayer journal

DATE _____

TODAY'S PASSAGE   PREACHER   SERMON TOPIC

NOTES
_____
_____
_____
_____
_____
_____
_____
_____
_____
_____
_____
_____
_____

KEY VERSES

PRAYER
_____
_____
_____
_____
_____
_____
_____

KEY POINTS

_____
_____
_____
_____
_____
_____
_____
_____
_____

APPLICATION

Prayer journal

DATE _____

TODAY'S PASSAGE   PREACHER   SERMON TOPIC

NOTES

_____
_____
_____
_____
_____
_____
_____
_____
_____
_____
_____

KEY VERSES

PRAYER

_____
_____
_____
_____
_____
_____

KEY POINTS

_____
_____
_____
_____
_____
_____
_____
_____

APPLICATION

DATE

Prayer journal

TODAY'S PASSAGE   PREACHER   SERMON TOPIC

NOTES

_____

_____

_____

_____

_____

_____

_____

_____

_____

_____

_____

KEY VERSES

PRAYER

_____

_____

_____

_____

_____

_____

_____

_____

_____

_____

_____

_____

_____

KEY POINTS

APPLICATION

Prayer journal

DATE _____

TODAY'S PASSAGE _____   PREACHER _____   SERMON TOPIC _____

NOTES
_____
_____
_____
_____
_____
_____
_____
_____
_____
_____
_____
_____
_____

KEY VERSES

PRAYER
_____
_____
_____
_____
_____
_____
_____

KEY POINTS

_____
_____
_____
_____
_____
_____
_____
_____

APPLICATION

Prayer journal

DATE _____

TODAY'S PASSAGE   PREACHER   SERMON TOPIC

NOTES
_____
_____
_____
_____
_____
_____
_____
_____
_____
_____

PRAYER
_____
_____
_____
_____
_____
_____
_____
_____
_____
_____
_____
_____
_____
_____

KEY VERSES

KEY POINTS

APPLICATION

Prayer journal

DATE

TODAY'S PASSAGE   PREACHER   SERMON TOPIC

NOTES

KEY VERSES

PRAYER

KEY POINTS

APPLICATION

Prayer journal

DATE _____

TODAY'S PASSAGE _____   PREACHER _____   SERMON TOPIC _____

NOTES
_____
_____
_____
_____
_____
_____
_____
_____
_____
_____
_____
_____

KEY VERSES

PRAYER
_____
_____
_____
_____
_____
_____
_____

KEY POINTS

_____
_____
_____
_____
_____
_____
_____
_____

APPLICATION

DATE _____

Prayer journal

TODAY'S PASSAGE   PREACHER   SERMON TOPIC

NOTES
_____

KEY VERSES

PRAYER
_____

KEY POINTS

APPLICATION

DATE _____

Prayer journal

TODAY'S PASSAGE   PREACHER   SERMON TOPIC

NOTES
_____
_____
_____
_____
_____
_____
_____
_____
_____
_____
_____

KEY VERSES

PRAYER
_____
_____
_____
_____
_____
_____

KEY POINTS

_____
_____
_____
_____
_____
_____
_____
_____
_____
_____

APPLICATION

Prayer journal

DATE _____

TODAY'S PASSAGE   PREACHER   SERMON TOPIC

NOTES
_____
_____
_____
_____
_____
_____
_____
_____
_____
_____

KEY VERSES

PRAYER
_____
_____
_____
_____
_____
_____

KEY POINTS

_____
_____
_____
_____
_____
_____
_____
_____

APPLICATION

Prayer journal

DATE

TODAY'S PASSAGE PREACHER SERMON TOPIC

NOTES

KEY VERSES

PRAYER

KEY POINTS

APPLICATION

Prayer journal

DATE _____

TODAY'S PASSAGE   PREACHER   SERMON TOPIC

NOTES
_____
_____
_____
_____
_____
_____
_____
_____
_____
_____
_____

KEY VERSES

PRAYER
_____
_____
_____
_____
_____

KEY POINTS

_____
_____
_____
_____
_____
_____
_____
_____

APPLICATION

Prayer journal

DATE _____

TODAY'S PASSAGE   PREACHER   SERMON TOPIC

NOTES

_____

_____

_____

_____

_____

_____

_____

_____

_____

_____

_____

_____

_____

KEY VERSES

PRAYER

_____

_____

_____

_____

_____

_____

KEY POINTS

_____

_____

_____

_____

_____

_____

_____

_____

_____

APPLICATION

Prayer journal

DATE _____

TODAY'S PASSAGE   PREACHER   SERMON TOPIC

NOTES

KEY VERSES

PRAYER

KEY POINTS

APPLICATION

DATE

Prayer journal

TODAY'S PASSAGE   PREACHER   SERMON TOPIC

NOTES

KEY VERSES

PRAYER

KEY POINTS

APPLICATION

Prayer journal

DATE _____

TODAY'S PASSAGE _____   PREACHER _____   SERMON TOPIC _____

NOTES
_____
_____
_____
_____
_____
_____
_____
_____
_____
_____
_____
_____

KEY VERSES

PRAYER
_____
_____
_____
_____
_____
_____

KEY POINTS

_____
_____
_____
_____
_____
_____
_____
_____
_____

APPLICATION

DATE _____

Prayer journal

TODAY'S PASSAGE   PREACHER   SERMON TOPIC

NOTES

_____
_____
_____
_____
_____
_____
_____
_____
_____
_____

PRAYER

_____
_____
_____
_____
_____

_____
_____
_____
_____
_____
_____
_____
_____

KEY VERSES

KEY POINTS

APPLICATION

Prayer journal

DATE _____

TODAY'S PASSAGE   PREACHER   SERMON TOPIC

NOTES
_____
_____
_____
_____
_____
_____
_____
_____
_____
_____
_____

PRAYER
_____
_____
_____
_____
_____
_____
_____
_____
_____
_____
_____
_____
_____
_____

KEY VERSES

KEY POINTS

APPLICATION

DATE _____

Prayer journal

TODAY'S PASSAGE   PREACHER   SERMON TOPIC

NOTES
_____
_____
_____
_____
_____
_____
_____
_____
_____
_____
_____
_____
_____

KEY VERSES

PRAYER
_____
_____
_____
_____
_____
_____
_____
_____
_____
_____
_____
_____
_____
_____

KEY POINTS

APPLICATION

Prayer journal

DATE _____

TODAY'S PASSAGE   PREACHER   SERMON TOPIC

NOTES

_____
_____
_____
_____
_____
_____
_____
_____
_____
_____
_____
_____

KEY VERSES

PRAYER

_____
_____
_____
_____
_____
_____
_____
_____
_____
_____
_____
_____
_____
_____
_____
_____

KEY POINTS

APPLICATION

Prayer journal

DATE

TODAY'S PASSAGE   PREACHER   SERMON TOPIC

NOTES

KEY VERSES

PRAYER

KEY POINTS

APPLICATION

Prayer journal

DATE _____

TODAY'S PASSAGE   PREACHER   SERMON TOPIC

NOTES
_____
_____
_____
_____
_____
_____
_____
_____
_____
_____
_____

KEY VERSES

PRAYER
_____
_____
_____
_____
_____

KEY POINTS

_____
_____
_____
_____
_____
_____
_____
_____
_____

APPLICATION

Prayer journal

DATE _____

TODAY'S PASSAGE   PREACHER   SERMON TOPIC

NOTES
_____
_____
_____
_____
_____
_____
_____
_____
_____
_____

KEY VERSES

PRAYER
_____
_____
_____
_____
_____
_____

KEY POINTS

_____
_____
_____
_____
_____
_____
_____
_____

APPLICATION

Prayer journal

DATE _____

TODAY'S PASSAGE _____ PREACHER _____ SERMON TOPIC _____

NOTES
_____
_____
_____
_____
_____
_____
_____
_____
_____
_____
_____
_____

KEY VERSES

PRAYER
_____
_____
_____
_____
_____
_____

KEY POINTS

_____
_____
_____
_____
_____
_____
_____
_____
_____

APPLICATION

Prayer journal

DATE

TODAY'S PASSAGE   PREACHER   SERMON TOPIC

NOTES

KEY VERSES

PRAYER

KEY POINTS

APPLICATION

Prayer journal

DATE _____

TODAY'S PASSAGE   PREACHER   SERMON TOPIC

NOTES
_____
_____
_____
_____
_____
_____
_____
_____
_____
_____

KEY VERSES

PRAYER
_____
_____
_____
_____
_____
_____
_____

KEY POINTS

_____
_____
_____
_____
_____
_____
_____
_____
_____

APPLICATION

Prayer journal

DATE _____

TODAY'S PASSAGE   PREACHER   SERMON TOPIC

NOTES
_____
_____
_____
_____
_____
_____
_____
_____
_____
_____
_____

KEY VERSES

PRAYER
_____
_____
_____
_____
_____
_____

KEY POINTS

_____
_____
_____
_____
_____
_____
_____
_____

APPLICATION

Prayer journal

DATE _____

TODAY'S PASSAGE _____   PREACHER _____   SERMON TOPIC _____

NOTES
_____
_____
_____
_____
_____
_____
_____
_____
_____
_____
_____
_____
_____

KEY VERSES

PRAYER
_____
_____
_____
_____
_____
_____
_____

KEY POINTS

_____
_____
_____
_____
_____
_____
_____
_____

APPLICATION

Prayer journal

DATE _____

TODAY'S PASSAGE   PREACHER   SERMON TOPIC

NOTES

_____

_____

_____

_____

_____

_____

_____

_____

_____

_____

KEY VERSES

PRAYER

_____

_____

_____

_____

_____

KEY POINTS

_____

_____

_____

_____

_____

_____

_____

APPLICATION

Prayer journal

DATE _____

TODAY'S PASSAGE   PREACHER   SERMON TOPIC

NOTES
_____
_____
_____
_____
_____
_____
_____
_____
_____
_____
_____
_____

PRAYER
_____
_____
_____
_____
_____
_____
_____
_____
_____
_____
_____
_____
_____
_____

KEY VERSES

KEY POINTS

APPLICATION

Prayer journal

DATE _____

TODAY'S PASSAGE   PREACHER   SERMON TOPIC

NOTES
_____
_____
_____
_____
_____
_____
_____
_____
_____
_____
_____

KEY VERSES

PRAYER
_____
_____
_____
_____
_____
_____

KEY POINTS

_____
_____
_____
_____
_____
_____
_____
_____

APPLICATION

Prayer journal

DATE _____

TODAY'S PASSAGE   PREACHER   SERMON TOPIC

NOTES
_____
_____
_____
_____
_____
_____
_____
_____
_____
_____
_____

KEY VERSES

PRAYER
_____
_____
_____
_____
_____
_____

KEY POINTS

_____
_____
_____
_____
_____
_____
_____
_____
_____

APPLICATION

Prayer journal

DATE _____

TODAY'S PASSAGE   PREACHER   SERMON TOPIC

NOTES
_____
_____
_____
_____
_____
_____
_____
_____
_____
_____
_____
_____

PRAYER
_____
_____
_____
_____
_____
_____
_____
_____
_____
_____
_____
_____
_____
_____

KEY VERSES

KEY POINTS

APPLICATION

Prayer journal

DATE

TODAY'S PASSAGE   PREACHER   SERMON TOPIC

NOTES

KEY VERSES

PRAYER

KEY POINTS

APPLICATION

DATE _____

Prayer journal

TODAY'S PASSAGE   PREACHER   SERMON TOPIC

NOTES
_____
_____
_____
_____
_____
_____
_____
_____
_____
_____

KEY VERSES

PRAYER
_____
_____
_____
_____
_____
_____

KEY POINTS

_____
_____
_____
_____
_____
_____
_____
_____
_____

APPLICATION

Prayer journal

DATE _____

TODAY'S PASSAGE   PREACHER   SERMON TOPIC

NOTES
_____
_____
_____
_____
_____
_____
_____
_____
_____
_____
_____
_____
_____

KEY VERSES

PRAYER
_____
_____
_____
_____
_____
_____
_____

KEY POINTS

_____
_____
_____
_____
_____
_____
_____
_____
_____
_____

APPLICATION

Prayer journal

DATE _____

TODAY'S PASSAGE   PREACHER   SERMON TOPIC

NOTES
_____
_____
_____
_____
_____
_____
_____
_____
_____
_____
_____

PRAYER
_____
_____
_____
_____
_____
_____
_____
_____
_____
_____
_____
_____
_____

KEY VERSES

KEY POINTS

APPLICATION

Prayer journal

DATE _____

TODAY'S PASSAGE   PREACHER   SERMON TOPIC

NOTES
_____
_____
_____
_____
_____
_____
_____
_____
_____
_____
_____
_____

KEY VERSES

PRAYER
_____
_____
_____
_____
_____
_____
_____
_____

KEY POINTS

_____
_____
_____
_____
_____
_____
_____
_____
_____

APPLICATION

Prayer journal

DATE _____

TODAY'S PASSAGE _____   PREACHER _____   SERMON TOPIC _____

NOTES
_____
_____
_____
_____
_____
_____
_____
_____
_____
_____
_____
_____

PRAYER
_____
_____
_____
_____
_____
_____
_____
_____
_____
_____
_____
_____
_____
_____
_____
_____

KEY VERSES

KEY POINTS

APPLICATION

Prayer journal

DATE _____

TODAY'S PASSAGE   PREACHER   SERMON TOPIC

NOTES
_____
_____
_____
_____
_____
_____
_____
_____
_____
_____
_____

PRAYER
_____
_____
_____
_____
_____
_____
_____
_____
_____
_____
_____
_____
_____
_____

KEY VERSES

KEY POINTS

APPLICATION

DATE _____

Prayer journal

TODAY'S PASSAGE _____   PREACHER _____   SERMON TOPIC _____

NOTES
_____
_____
_____
_____
_____
_____
_____
_____
_____
_____
_____

KEY VERSES

PRAYER
_____
_____
_____
_____
_____
_____

KEY POINTS

_____
_____
_____
_____
_____
_____
_____
_____
_____

APPLICATION

Prayer journal

DATE _____

TODAY'S PASSAGE   PREACHER   SERMON TOPIC

NOTES
_____
_____
_____
_____
_____
_____
_____
_____
_____
_____
_____
_____

PRAYER
_____
_____
_____
_____
_____
_____
_____
_____
_____
_____
_____
_____
_____
_____
_____
_____

KEY VERSES

KEY POINTS

APPLICATION

Prayer journal

DATE _____

TODAY'S PASSAGE _____   PREACHER _____   SERMON TOPIC _____

NOTES
_____
_____
_____
_____
_____
_____
_____
_____
_____
_____
_____
_____
_____

KEY VERSES

PRAYER
_____
_____
_____
_____
_____
_____
_____

KEY POINTS

_____
_____
_____
_____
_____
_____
_____
_____

APPLICATION

Prayer journal

DATE _____

TODAY'S PASSAGE   PREACHER   SERMON TOPIC

NOTES
_____
_____
_____
_____
_____
_____
_____
_____
_____
_____
_____

KEY VERSES

PRAYER
_____
_____
_____
_____
_____
_____

KEY POINTS

_____
_____
_____
_____
_____
_____
_____
_____

APPLICATION

Prayer journal

DATE _____

TODAY'S PASSAGE   PREACHER   SERMON TOPIC

NOTES
_____
_____
_____
_____
_____
_____
_____
_____
_____
_____
_____

KEY VERSES

PRAYER
_____
_____
_____
_____
_____
_____

KEY POINTS

_____
_____
_____
_____
_____
_____
_____
_____
_____
_____

APPLICATION

Prayer journal

DATE _____

TODAY'S PASSAGE   PREACHER   SERMON TOPIC

NOTES
_____
_____
_____
_____
_____
_____
_____
_____
_____
_____
_____
_____

KEY VERSES

PRAYER
_____
_____
_____
_____
_____

KEY POINTS

_____
_____
_____
_____
_____
_____
_____
_____
_____

APPLICATION

DATE _____

Prayer journal

TODAY'S PASSAGE   PREACHER   SERMON TOPIC

NOTES
_____
_____
_____
_____
_____
_____
_____
_____
_____
_____
_____
_____

KEY VERSES

PRAYER
_____
_____
_____
_____
_____
_____

KEY POINTS

_____
_____
_____
_____
_____
_____
_____
_____
_____

APPLICATION

Prayer journal

DATE _____

TODAY'S PASSAGE   PREACHER   SERMON TOPIC

NOTES
_____
_____
_____
_____
_____
_____
_____
_____
_____
_____
_____

PRAYER
_____
_____
_____
_____
_____
_____
_____
_____
_____
_____
_____
_____
_____

KEY VERSES

KEY POINTS

APPLICATION

Prayer journal

DATE _____

TODAY'S PASSAGE   PREACHER   SERMON TOPIC

NOTES
_____
_____
_____
_____
_____
_____
_____
_____
_____
_____
_____
_____
_____

KEY VERSES

PRAYER
_____
_____
_____
_____
_____
_____

KEY POINTS

_____
_____
_____
_____
_____
_____
_____
_____

APPLICATION

Prayer journal

DATE _____

TODAY'S PASSAGE   PREACHER   SERMON TOPIC

NOTES
_____
_____
_____
_____
_____
_____
_____
_____
_____
_____
_____
_____

KEY VERSES

PRAYER
_____
_____
_____
_____
_____
_____

KEY POINTS

_____
_____
_____
_____
_____
_____
_____
_____

APPLICATION

Prayer journal

DATE _____

TODAY'S PASSAGE   PREACHER   SERMON TOPIC

NOTES
_____
_____
_____
_____
_____
_____
_____
_____
_____
_____
_____
_____

KEY VERSES

PRAYER
_____
_____
_____
_____
_____
_____

KEY POINTS

_____
_____
_____
_____
_____
_____
_____
_____
_____

APPLICATION

Prayer journal

DATE _____

TODAY'S PASSAGE   PREACHER   SERMON TOPIC

NOTES
_____
_____
_____
_____
_____
_____
_____
_____
_____
_____
_____

KEY VERSES

PRAYER
_____
_____
_____
_____
_____
_____

KEY POINTS

_____
_____
_____
_____
_____
_____
_____
_____
_____

APPLICATION

DATE _____ # Prayer journal

TODAY'S PASSAGE   PREACHER   SERMON TOPIC

NOTES
_____
_____
_____
_____
_____
_____
_____
_____
_____
_____
_____

PRAYER
_____
_____
_____
_____
_____
_____
_____
_____
_____
_____
_____
_____
_____
_____
_____

KEY VERSES

KEY POINTS

APPLICATION

Prayer journal

DATE _____

TODAY'S PASSAGE   PREACHER   SERMON TOPIC

NOTES
_____
_____
_____
_____
_____
_____
_____
_____
_____
_____
_____
_____
_____

KEY VERSES

PRAYER
_____
_____
_____
_____
_____
_____

KEY POINTS

_____
_____
_____
_____
_____
_____
_____
_____
_____

APPLICATION

Prayer journal

DATE

TODAY'S PASSAGE   PREACHER   SERMON TOPIC

NOTES

KEY VERSES

PRAYER

KEY POINTS

APPLICATION

DATE _____

Prayer journal

TODAY'S PASSAGE   PREACHER   SERMON TOPIC

NOTES

_____

_____

_____

_____

_____

_____

_____

_____

_____

_____

KEY VERSES

PRAYER

_____

_____

_____

_____

_____

KEY POINTS

_____

_____

_____

_____

_____

_____

_____

APPLICATION

DATE _____

Prayer journal

TODAY'S PASSAGE   PREACHER   SERMON TOPIC

NOTES
_____
_____
_____
_____
_____
_____
_____
_____
_____
_____
_____

KEY VERSES

PRAYER
_____
_____
_____
_____
_____
_____

KEY POINTS

_____
_____
_____
_____
_____
_____
_____
_____
_____
_____

APPLICATION

Prayer journal

DATE _____

TODAY'S PASSAGE   PREACHER   SERMON TOPIC

NOTES
_____
_____
_____
_____
_____
_____
_____
_____
_____
_____
_____
_____

PRAYER
_____
_____
_____
_____
_____
_____
_____
_____
_____
_____
_____
_____
_____
_____

KEY VERSES

KEY POINTS

APPLICATION

Prayer journal

DATE _____

TODAY'S PASSAGE   PREACHER   SERMON TOPIC

NOTES
_____
_____
_____
_____
_____
_____
_____
_____
_____
_____
_____

KEY VERSES

PRAYER
_____
_____
_____
_____
_____

KEY POINTS

_____
_____
_____
_____
_____
_____
_____
_____
_____

APPLICATION

DATE _____

Prayer journal

TODAY'S PASSAGE   PREACHER   SERMON TOPIC

NOTES
_____
_____
_____
_____
_____
_____
_____
_____
_____
_____
_____
_____
_____

KEY VERSES

PRAYER
_____
_____
_____
_____
_____
_____
_____
_____
_____
_____
_____
_____
_____
_____
_____
_____

KEY POINTS

APPLICATION

Prayer journal

DATE _____

TODAY'S PASSAGE   PREACHER   SERMON TOPIC

NOTES
_____
_____
_____
_____
_____
_____
_____
_____
_____
_____
_____
_____

KEY VERSES

PRAYER
_____
_____
_____
_____
_____

KEY POINTS

_____
_____
_____
_____
_____
_____
_____

APPLICATION

Prayer journal

DATE _____

TODAY'S PASSAGE _____ PREACHER _____ SERMON TOPIC _____

NOTES
_____
_____
_____
_____
_____
_____
_____
_____
_____
_____
_____

KEY VERSES

PRAYER
_____
_____
_____
_____
_____
_____

KEY POINTS

_____
_____
_____
_____
_____
_____
_____
_____

APPLICATION

Prayer journal

DATE _____

TODAY'S PASSAGE   PREACHER   SERMON TOPIC

NOTES
_____
_____
_____
_____
_____
_____
_____
_____
_____
_____
_____

KEY VERSES

PRAYER
_____
_____
_____
_____
_____
_____

KEY POINTS

_____
_____
_____
_____
_____
_____
_____
_____
_____
_____

APPLICATION

Prayer journal

DATE _____

TODAY'S PASSAGE   PREACHER   SERMON TOPIC

NOTES
_____
_____
_____
_____
_____
_____
_____
_____
_____
_____
_____
_____

KEY VERSES

PRAYER
_____
_____
_____
_____
_____
_____

KEY POINTS

_____
_____
_____
_____
_____
_____
_____
_____

APPLICATION

DATE _____

Prayer journal

TODAY'S PASSAGE   PREACHER   SERMON TOPIC

NOTES
_____
_____
_____
_____
_____
_____
_____
_____
_____
_____
_____

PRAYER
_____
_____
_____
_____
_____
_____

_____
_____
_____
_____
_____
_____
_____
_____
_____

KEY VERSES

KEY POINTS

APPLICATION

Prayer journal

DATE _____

TODAY'S PASSAGE   PREACHER   SERMON TOPIC

NOTES

_____
_____
_____
_____
_____
_____
_____
_____
_____
_____
_____

KEY VERSES

PRAYER

_____
_____
_____
_____
_____
_____
_____
_____
_____
_____
_____
_____
_____
_____

KEY POINTS

APPLICATION

Prayer journal

DATE _____

TODAY'S PASSAGE   PREACHER   SERMON TOPIC

NOTES
_____
_____
_____
_____
_____
_____
_____
_____
_____
_____
_____
_____

KEY VERSES

PRAYER
_____
_____
_____
_____
_____
_____

KEY POINTS

_____
_____
_____
_____
_____
_____
_____
_____
_____

APPLICATION

Prayer journal

DATE _____

TODAY'S PASSAGE   PREACHER   SERMON TOPIC

NOTES
_____
_____
_____
_____
_____
_____
_____
_____
_____
_____
_____

PRAYER
_____
_____
_____
_____
_____
_____
_____
_____
_____
_____
_____
_____
_____
_____

KEY VERSES

KEY POINTS

APPLICATION

DATE

Prayer journal

TODAY'S PASSAGE   PREACHER   SERMON TOPIC

NOTES

KEY VERSES

PRAYER

KEY POINTS

APPLICATION

Prayer journal

DATE _____

TODAY'S PASSAGE   PREACHER   SERMON TOPIC

NOTES
_____
_____
_____
_____
_____
_____
_____
_____
_____
_____
_____
_____

PRAYER
_____
_____
_____
_____
_____
_____
_____
_____
_____
_____
_____
_____
_____
_____

KEY VERSES

KEY POINTS

APPLICATION

Prayer journal

DATE _____

TODAY'S PASSAGE   PREACHER   SERMON TOPIC

NOTES
_____
_____
_____
_____
_____
_____
_____
_____
_____
_____

PRAYER
_____
_____
_____
_____
_____
_____

_____
_____
_____
_____
_____
_____
_____

KEY VERSES

KEY POINTS

APPLICATION

DATE _____

Prayer journal

TODAY'S PASSAGE   PREACHER   SERMON TOPIC

NOTES
_____
_____
_____
_____
_____
_____
_____
_____
_____
_____
_____
_____

KEY VERSES

PRAYER
_____
_____
_____
_____
_____
_____

KEY POINTS

_____
_____
_____
_____
_____
_____
_____
_____
_____
_____

APPLICATION

Prayer journal

DATE _____

TODAY'S PASSAGE   PREACHER   SERMON TOPIC

NOTES
_____
_____
_____
_____
_____
_____
_____
_____
_____

KEY VERSES

PRAYER
_____
_____
_____
_____
_____

KEY POINTS

_____
_____
_____
_____
_____
_____
_____

APPLICATION

Prayer journal

DATE _____

TODAY'S PASSAGE   PREACHER   SERMON TOPIC

NOTES
_____
_____
_____
_____
_____
_____
_____
_____
_____
_____
_____
_____

KEY VERSES

PRAYER
_____
_____
_____
_____
_____
_____

KEY POINTS

_____
_____
_____
_____
_____
_____
_____
_____

APPLICATION

Prayer journal

DATE _____

TODAY'S PASSAGE   PREACHER   SERMON TOPIC

NOTES
_____
_____
_____
_____
_____
_____
_____
_____
_____
_____
_____

PRAYER
_____
_____
_____
_____
_____
_____
_____
_____
_____
_____
_____
_____
_____
_____

KEY VERSES

KEY POINTS

APPLICATION

Prayer journal

DATE _____

TODAY'S PASSAGE _____   PREACHER _____   SERMON TOPIC _____

NOTES
_____
_____
_____
_____
_____
_____
_____
_____
_____
_____

KEY VERSES

PRAYER
_____
_____
_____
_____
_____
_____

KEY POINTS

_____
_____
_____
_____
_____
_____
_____
_____
_____

APPLICATION

DATE _____

Prayer journal

TODAY'S PASSAGE   PREACHER   SERMON TOPIC

NOTES
_____
_____
_____
_____
_____
_____
_____
_____
_____
_____
_____

KEY VERSES

PRAYER
_____
_____
_____
_____
_____
_____

KEY POINTS

_____
_____
_____
_____
_____
_____
_____
_____
_____

APPLICATION

Prayer journal

DATE _____

TODAY'S PASSAGE | PREACHER | SERMON TOPIC

NOTES
_____
_____
_____
_____
_____
_____
_____
_____
_____
_____
_____
_____
_____

KEY VERSES

PRAYER
_____
_____
_____
_____
_____
_____
_____

KEY POINTS

_____
_____
_____
_____
_____
_____
_____
_____
_____
_____
_____

APPLICATION

DATE _____

Prayer journal

TODAY'S PASSAGE   PREACHER   SERMON TOPIC

NOTES
_____
_____
_____
_____
_____
_____
_____
_____
_____
_____
_____

KEY VERSES

PRAYER
_____
_____
_____
_____
_____
_____

KEY POINTS

_____
_____
_____
_____
_____
_____
_____

APPLICATION

Prayer journal

DATE

TODAY'S PASSAGE   PREACHER   SERMON TOPIC

NOTES

KEY VERSES

KEY POINTS

PRAYER

APPLICATION

Prayer journal

DATE _____

TODAY'S PASSAGE _____ PREACHER _____ SERMON TOPIC _____

NOTES
_____
_____
_____
_____
_____
_____
_____
_____
_____
_____
_____
_____

KEY VERSES

PRAYER
_____
_____
_____
_____
_____
_____

KEY POINTS

_____
_____
_____
_____
_____
_____
_____
_____

APPLICATION

Prayer journal

DATE _____

TODAY'S PASSAGE   PREACHER   SERMON TOPIC

NOTES

KEY VERSES

PRAYER

KEY POINTS

APPLICATION

DATE _____

Prayer journal

TODAY'S PASSAGE _____ PREACHER _____ SERMON TOPIC _____

NOTES
_____
_____
_____
_____
_____
_____
_____
_____
_____
_____
_____

KEY VERSES

PRAYER
_____
_____
_____
_____
_____
_____

KEY POINTS

_____
_____
_____
_____
_____
_____
_____
_____

APPLICATION

Prayer journal

DATE _____

TODAY'S PASSAGE   PREACHER   SERMON TOPIC

NOTES
_____
_____
_____
_____
_____
_____
_____
_____
_____
_____
_____

PRAYER
_____
_____
_____
_____
_____
_____
_____
_____
_____
_____
_____
_____
_____
_____

KEY VERSES

KEY POINTS

APPLICATION

Prayer journal

DATE _____

TODAY'S PASSAGE   PREACHER   SERMON TOPIC

NOTES
_____
_____
_____
_____
_____
_____
_____
_____
_____
_____
_____

KEY VERSES

PRAYER
_____
_____
_____
_____
_____
_____

KEY POINTS

_____
_____
_____
_____
_____
_____
_____
_____

APPLICATION

DATE _____

Prayer journal

TODAY'S PASSAGE   PREACHER   SERMON TOPIC

NOTES
_____
_____
_____
_____
_____
_____
_____
_____
_____
_____
_____
_____

KEY VERSES

PRAYER
_____
_____
_____
_____
_____
_____
_____

KEY POINTS

_____
_____
_____
_____
_____
_____
_____
_____

APPLICATION

DATE _____

Prayer journal

TODAY'S PASSAGE   PREACHER   SERMON TOPIC

NOTES
_____
_____
_____
_____
_____
_____
_____
_____
_____
_____
_____
_____

PRAYER
_____
_____
_____
_____
_____
_____
_____
_____
_____
_____
_____
_____
_____

KEY VERSES

KEY POINTS

APPLICATION

DATE _____

Prayer journal

TODAY'S PASSAGE   PREACHER   SERMON TOPIC

NOTES

KEY VERSES

PRAYER

KEY POINTS

APPLICATION

DATE

Prayer journal

TODAY'S PASSAGE   PREACHER   SERMON TOPIC

NOTES

KEY VERSES

PRAYER

KEY POINTS

APPLICATION

Prayer journal

DATE _____

TODAY'S PASSAGE   PREACHER   SERMON TOPIC

NOTES
_____
_____
_____
_____
_____
_____
_____
_____
_____
_____
_____
_____

KEY VERSES

PRAYER
_____
_____
_____
_____
_____
_____

KEY POINTS

_____
_____
_____
_____
_____
_____
_____
_____
_____

APPLICATION

Prayer journal

DATE _____

TODAY'S PASSAGE _____ PREACHER _____ SERMON TOPIC _____

NOTES
_____
_____
_____
_____
_____
_____
_____
_____
_____
_____
_____

KEY VERSES

PRAYER
_____
_____
_____
_____
_____

KEY POINTS

_____
_____
_____
_____
_____
_____
_____

APPLICATION

Prayer journal

DATE _____

TODAY'S PASSAGE   PREACHER   SERMON TOPIC

NOTES

_____
_____
_____
_____
_____
_____
_____
_____
_____
_____
_____
_____

PRAYER

_____
_____
_____
_____
_____
_____
_____
_____
_____
_____
_____
_____
_____
_____
_____
_____

KEY VERSES

KEY POINTS

APPLICATION

DATE _____

Prayer journal

TODAY'S PASSAGE   PREACHER   SERMON TOPIC

NOTES
_____
_____
_____
_____
_____
_____
_____
_____
_____
_____
_____

KEY VERSES

PRAYER
_____
_____
_____
_____
_____
_____

KEY POINTS

_____
_____
_____
_____
_____
_____
_____
_____
_____

APPLICATION

Prayer journal

DATE _____

TODAY'S PASSAGE   PREACHER   SERMON TOPIC

NOTES
_____
_____
_____
_____
_____
_____
_____
_____
_____
_____
_____

KEY VERSES

PRAYER
_____
_____
_____
_____
_____
_____

KEY POINTS

_____
_____
_____
_____
_____
_____
_____
_____
_____

APPLICATION

DATE _____

Prayer journal

TODAY'S PASSAGE   PREACHER   SERMON TOPIC

NOTES
_____
_____
_____
_____
_____
_____
_____
_____
_____
_____
_____

PRAYER
_____
_____
_____
_____
_____
_____

_____
_____
_____
_____
_____
_____
_____
_____

KEY VERSES

KEY POINTS

APPLICATION

Prayer journal

DATE _____

TODAY'S PASSAGE   PREACHER   SERMON TOPIC

NOTES
_____
_____
_____
_____
_____
_____
_____
_____
_____
_____
_____

KEY VERSES

PRAYER
_____
_____
_____
_____
_____
_____

KEY POINTS

_____
_____
_____
_____
_____
_____
_____
_____

APPLICATION

Prayer journal

DATE _____

TODAY'S PASSAGE   PREACHER   SERMON TOPIC

NOTES
_____
_____
_____
_____
_____
_____
_____
_____
_____
_____
_____

PRAYER
_____
_____
_____
_____
_____
_____
_____
_____
_____
_____
_____
_____

KEY VERSES

KEY POINTS

APPLICATION

Prayer journal

DATE _____

TODAY'S PASSAGE   PREACHER   SERMON TOPIC

NOTES
_____
_____
_____
_____
_____
_____
_____
_____
_____
_____
_____
_____

KEY VERSES

PRAYER
_____
_____
_____
_____
_____
_____

KEY POINTS

_____
_____
_____
_____
_____
_____
_____
_____
_____

APPLICATION

Prayer journal

DATE _____

TODAY'S PASSAGE   PREACHER   SERMON TOPIC

NOTES
_____
_____
_____
_____
_____
_____
_____
_____
_____
_____
_____

PRAYER
_____
_____
_____
_____
_____
_____
_____
_____
_____
_____
_____
_____
_____

KEY VERSES

KEY POINTS

APPLICATION

DATE

Prayer journal

TODAY'S PASSAGE   PREACHER   SERMON TOPIC

NOTES

KEY VERSES

PRAYER

KEY POINTS

APPLICATION

DATE _____

Prayer journal

TODAY'S PASSAGE   PREACHER   SERMON TOPIC

NOTES
_____
_____
_____
_____
_____
_____
_____
_____
_____
_____
_____

KEY VERSES

PRAYER
_____
_____
_____
_____
_____
_____

KEY POINTS

_____
_____
_____
_____
_____
_____
_____
_____

APPLICATION

Prayer journal

DATE _____

TODAY'S PASSAGE   PREACHER   SERMON TOPIC

NOTES
_____
_____
_____
_____
_____
_____
_____
_____
_____
_____
_____
_____

PRAYER
_____
_____
_____
_____
_____
_____
_____
_____
_____
_____
_____
_____
_____
_____
_____
_____

KEY VERSES

KEY POINTS

APPLICATION

Prayer journal

DATE _____

TODAY'S PASSAGE   PREACHER   SERMON TOPIC

NOTES
_____

KEY VERSES

_____

KEY POINTS

PRAYER
_____

APPLICATION

Prayer journal

DATE _____

TODAY'S PASSAGE   PREACHER   SERMON TOPIC

NOTES
_____
_____
_____
_____
_____
_____
_____
_____
_____
_____
_____

KEY VERSES

PRAYER
_____
_____
_____
_____
_____
_____

KEY POINTS

_____
_____
_____
_____
_____
_____
_____
_____

APPLICATION

DATE _____

Prayer journal

TODAY'S PASSAGE   PREACHER   SERMON TOPIC

NOTES
_____
_____
_____
_____
_____
_____
_____
_____
_____
_____
_____

KEY VERSES

PRAYER
_____
_____
_____
_____
_____
_____

KEY POINTS

_____
_____
_____
_____
_____
_____
_____
_____
_____

APPLICATION

Prayer journal

DATE _____

TODAY'S PASSAGE   PREACHER   SERMON TOPIC

NOTES
_____
_____
_____
_____
_____
_____
_____
_____
_____
_____
_____

KEY VERSES

PRAYER
_____
_____
_____
_____
_____
_____
_____

KEY POINTS

_____
_____
_____
_____
_____
_____
_____
_____
_____

APPLICATION

DATE _____

Prayer journal

TODAY'S PASSAGE   PREACHER   SERMON TOPIC

NOTES
_____
_____
_____
_____
_____
_____
_____
_____
_____
_____
_____

KEY VERSES

PRAYER
_____
_____
_____
_____
_____

KEY POINTS

_____
_____
_____
_____
_____
_____
_____
_____
_____

APPLICATION

Prayer journal

DATE _____

TODAY'S PASSAGE   PREACHER   SERMON TOPIC

NOTES
_____
_____
_____
_____
_____
_____
_____
_____
_____
_____
_____

KEY VERSES

PRAYER
_____
_____
_____
_____
_____

KEY POINTS

_____
_____
_____
_____
_____
_____
_____
_____
_____

APPLICATION

Prayer journal

DATE _____

TODAY'S PASSAGE   PREACHER   SERMON TOPIC

NOTES
_____
_____
_____
_____
_____
_____
_____
_____
_____
_____
_____
_____

KEY VERSES

PRAYER
_____
_____
_____
_____
_____

KEY POINTS

_____
_____
_____
_____
_____
_____
_____
_____

APPLICATION

Prayer journal

DATE _____

TODAY'S PASSAGE   PREACHER   SERMON TOPIC

NOTES
_____
_____
_____
_____
_____
_____
_____
_____
_____
_____
_____

PRAYER
_____
_____
_____
_____
_____
_____
_____
_____
_____
_____
_____
_____
_____

KEY VERSES

KEY POINTS

APPLICATION

Prayer journal

DATE _____

TODAY'S PASSAGE   PREACHER   SERMON TOPIC

NOTES
_____
_____
_____
_____
_____
_____
_____
_____
_____
_____
_____

KEY VERSES

PRAYER
_____
_____
_____
_____
_____
_____

KEY POINTS

_____
_____
_____
_____
_____
_____
_____
_____

APPLICATION

Prayer journal

DATE _____

TODAY'S PASSAGE   PREACHER   SERMON TOPIC

NOTES
_____
_____
_____
_____
_____
_____
_____
_____
_____
_____
_____

PRAYER
_____
_____
_____
_____
_____
_____

_____
_____
_____
_____
_____
_____
_____
_____

KEY VERSES

KEY POINTS

APPLICATION

DATE _____

Prayer journal

TODAY'S PASSAGE _____ PREACHER _____ SERMON TOPIC _____

NOTES

_____
_____
_____
_____
_____
_____
_____
_____
_____
_____
_____
_____

KEY VERSES

PRAYER

_____
_____
_____
_____
_____
_____

KEY POINTS

_____
_____
_____
_____
_____
_____
_____
_____
_____

APPLICATION

Prayer journal

DATE _____

TODAY'S PASSAGE _____   PREACHER _____   SERMON TOPIC _____

NOTES
_____
_____
_____
_____
_____
_____
_____
_____
_____
_____
_____

KEY VERSES

PRAYER
_____
_____
_____
_____
_____
_____

KEY POINTS

_____
_____
_____
_____
_____
_____
_____
_____
_____

APPLICATION

Prayer journal

DATE _____

TODAY'S PASSAGE   PREACHER   SERMON TOPIC

NOTES

_____

_____

_____

_____

_____

_____

_____

_____

_____

_____

_____

PRAYER

_____

_____

_____

_____

_____

_____

_____

_____

_____

_____

_____

KEY VERSES

KEY POINTS

APPLICATION

Prayer journal

DATE _____

TODAY'S PASSAGE   PREACHER   SERMON TOPIC

NOTES
_____
_____
_____
_____
_____
_____
_____
_____
_____
_____
_____

KEY VERSES

PRAYER
_____
_____
_____
_____
_____
_____

KEY POINTS

_____
_____
_____
_____
_____
_____
_____
_____

APPLICATION

Prayer journal

DATE

TODAY'S PASSAGE   PREACHER   SERMON TOPIC

NOTES

KEY VERSES

PRAYER

KEY POINTS

APPLICATION

Prayer journal

DATE _____

TODAY'S PASSAGE   PREACHER   SERMON TOPIC

NOTES

_____
_____
_____
_____
_____
_____
_____
_____
_____
_____
_____

KEY VERSES

PRAYER

_____
_____
_____
_____
_____
_____
_____
_____
_____
_____
_____
_____
_____
_____
_____

KEY POINTS

APPLICATION

Made in the USA
Las Vegas, NV
19 September 2024

95495248R00069